LOOK WHO'S GOING TO SCHOOL!

Building confidence, Kindness and Helping Children with Separation Anxiety

Written by –
ROSEANNE HINCH

**COPYRIGHT © 2025 ROSEANNE HINCH
ALL RIGHTS RESERVED**

No part of this publication shall be reproduced, transmitted, or sold in whole or in part in any form without prior written consent of the author, except as provided by the United States of America copyright law. Any unauthorized usage of text without express written permission of the publisher is in violation of the authors copyright and is illegal and punishable by law. All trademarks and registered trademarks appearing in this guide are the property of their respective owners.
Roseanne Hinch.

PAPERBACK ISBN: 979-8-218-58424-5
HARDCOVER ISBN: 979-8-218-56711-8

Printed in United states of America First Addition 2025.

DEDICATION

To our grandson, Grayson, as you are getting ready for kindergarten, the first day of school is the first step in your great adventure. You are BRAVE!
- Love, Nawney

AUTHOR PAGE

Award Winning Children's Author Roseanne Hinch lives in Maryland with her husband. She runs a small child care business with over 29 years' experience working with children of all ages. Her first children's book "When Mommy Drops me off at School" helps children with separation anxiety. Roseanne is passionate about helping children grow and their families.
Look for all of her books @ Roseannehinch.com

TABLE OF CONTENTS

CHAPTER 1
SHARING WITH FRIENDS AT SCHOOL...............1

CHAPTER 2
LUNCH TIME AT SCHOOL........................11

CHAPTER 3
MS. SALLY'S BUS # 205........................23

CHAPTER 1
SHARING WITH FRIENDS AT SCHOOL

When I go to school, and it's my helper day,
I get so excited because I get to pick out what we will play.

When I'm at home, I can play with my mommy and daddy;
When I'm at school, I have to share even with my friend Maddie.

It's hard for me even though I know sharing is the right thing to do,
When I see a really cool toy, I want to cry BOO HOO!

My teacher said I can ask my friend, "May I have that toy next".
I'll see how much fun it is to be a good friend and sharing is always the best.

Today when I go to my center and play, I'll remember to ask to be next to play with that toy.
I can share with my friends and play together, that would be such a big joy.

When I share with my friends, the fun never ends. I always learn so much more,
To share is so golden not just for 1 but maybe friends 2, 3, and 4.

The next time it's share day I'm going to be so excited,
For sharing is nice, and sharing is fun, especially when you are invited.

Sharing at school is now the best thing ever, I know this now to be true.
Whether it's my helper day or not, I'll be the best SHARE friend at my school.

Some days it's okay to play by myself, for I learn and grow deep inside.

Sometimes it looks different you see; we are all here to enjoy the ride.

THE END

CHAPTER 2
LUNCH TIME AT SCHOOL

Having lunch at my school is fun for me, I sit with my whole class at one time.

No matter which friends are there, I can't wait to hear the bells chime.

It's important to know all the rules about getting ready, you see.
I use the restroom and wash my hands. I make sure I use soap, it's the key.

I sit nice and tall and roll up my sleeves. I am ready. I find my lunch chair, place my hands on my lap, and sit with my feet on the floor, nice and steady.

Waiting for my lunch is a great part of my day. I can't wait to see what we will have that will be so yummy.

I'm served from each food group: dairy, fruits, vegetables, grains, and protein, too.

I can't wait for it to reach my tummy.

My lunch is finally here. I'm excited to eat, but first I must wait.

We will be served one by one on each individual plate.

Because I'm not at home, the lunch here maybe a little different than I'm used to.

Eating with my friends, it feels so special, and sometimes it's loud like a ZOO!

Everyone has been served. We all washed our hands, our hands on our laps, our feet on the floor. Now we can eat, and when we are done, we can always ask for more.

When I'm finished with my lunch, I clean up my space,

I'm not in a hurry, and I know this is not a race.

Tomorrow I'll do this all over again.

I'll be ready for lunch, and I'll be able to sit with my friend.

CHAPTER 3
MS. SALLY'S BUS # 205

I'm so excited to ride the bus when I go to school.
It's so big and tall, I wonder if I'll need a stool.

I have never gone on a real school bus ride,
I'm going to be brave and try not to cry.

Bus #205 arrives at my bus stop; the door opens wide.

Ms. Sally, the driver, she welcomes me with pride.

I'm scared, and I'm worried. My mom tells me I'll be okay.

Ms. Sally greets each one of us in a special kind of way.

I find an empty seat all by myself, sit alone, and I feel worried.

I see a lot of kids walking up and down the aisle as they scurry.

Ms. Sally noticed that I'm all by myself, sad and alone,

Ms. Sally walks right over to me full of kindness that she has shown.

Ms. Sally asked a friend to sit with me and become my "Bus Buddy,"
Now I'm feeling much brighter, and my heart is not so muddy.

Tomorrow when I go to school, I'll be waiting for bus #205.
I know Ms. Sally will be at my bus stop, so I'll be ready for a ride.

I'll sit with my "Bus Buddy". We can sing and share and talk.

As we all ride on Ms. Sally's bus # 205, together this year we will ROCK!

THE END

Showing Kindness

www.ingramcontent.com/pod-product-compliance
Lightning Source LLC
Chambersburg PA
CBHW042052050526
44107CB00109B/1090